ZEBRAS

by Jenny Markert

Published in the United States of America by The Child's World®
1980 Lookout Drive • Mankato, MN 56003-1705
800-599-READ • www.childsworld.com

PHOTO CREDITS
© Adam Jones/Visuals Unlimited: 12
© Ann and Steve Toon/Alamy: cover, 1
© blickwinkel/Alamy: 27
© Clem Haagner; Gallo Images/Corbis: 15
© Frans Lanting/Minden Pictures: 7
© Karl Ammann/Corbis: 16
© Martin Harvey/Corbis: 10–11
© mediacolor's/Alamy: 20–21
© Richard Du Toit/naturepl.com: 4–5
© Steve Bloom Images/Alamy: 22
© Stuart Westmorland/Getty Images: 19
© Tim Graham/Alamy: 9
© Wendy Dennis/Visuals Unlimited: 29
© WorldFoto/Alamy: 25

ACKNOWLEDGMENTS
The Child's World®: Mary Berendes, Publishing Director;
Katherine Stevenson, Editor; Pamela Mitsakos, Photo Researcher;
Judy Karren, Fact Checker

The Design Lab: Kathleen Petelinsek, Design and Page Production

LIBRARY OF CONGRESS CATALOGING-IN-PUBLICATION DATA
Markert, Jenny.
  Zebras / by Jenny Markert.
      p. cm. — (New naturebooks)
  Includes index.
  ISBN-13: 978-1-59296-854-1 (library bound : alk. paper)
  ISBN-10: 1-59296-854-6 (library bound : alk. paper)
  1. Zebras—Juvenile literature. I. Title.
  QL737.U62M37 2007
  599.665'7—dc22   2006103446

Table of Contents

On the cover: These Burchell's zebras live in South Africa's Mkuze game reserve.

Meet the Zebra!

Zebras don't make very good pets. But people have mated zebras with horses and donkeys to try to make better pets. A zebra/horse mix is called a *zorse*. A zebra/pony mix is a *zony*. A zebra/donkey mix is a *zebrass* or *zedonk*.

The hot afternoon sun beats down on the African plain. In the distance a herd of animals stands grazing in the tall grass. They look a lot like horses— but they're not black or brown or white like regular horses. Instead, they have bold black and white stripes all over their bodies. What are these colorful animals? They're zebras!

These Burchell's zebras are visiting a water hole in Botswana's Chobe National Park.

4

What Are Zebras?

Donkeys and onagers are members of the horse family, too.

Underneath its striped coat, a zebra's skin is dark.

The main predators that hunt zebras are lions. Hyenas, leopards, cheetahs, and hunting dogs attack them, too.

Zebras are members of the horse family that live in Africa. Like other horses, they're warm-bodied, fur-covered **mammals** with long bodies and four strong legs. Their feet have hard, sturdy hooves that help them run fast and protect themselves. But zebras look different from their other horse relatives. Their manes stick straight up, and their tails have tufts of hair on the tips. And they have stripes—lots of them! Most zebras are covered with black and white stripes. Some have brown stripes.

This Burchell's zebra is keeping a close eye on the photographer. Its ears are pointed forward so it can listen for any signs of danger.

Are There Different Kinds of Zebras?

Zebras of different species cannot mate with each other successfully. Even if they produce a baby, it can't have babies of its own.

Plains zebras make an unusual barking sound.

Two kinds of plains zebras are now extinct. One kind, the quagga, was yellowish brown and had stripes only on its front half.

There are three basic kinds, or **species**, of zebras. The ones we know best are plains zebras, also called common zebras or Burchell's zebras. Plains zebras are built like sturdy ponies. They stand 47 to 55 inches (119 to 140 cm) tall at the shoulder and weigh up to 660 pounds (299 kg). They tend to have up-and-down stripes on their sides and wide, sideways stripes on their back ends. The plains zebra's stripes go up into its short mane and all the way around its belly. Its short, striped legs end in wide hooves. There are several types, or *subspecies*, of plains zebras. The most common and best known are Grant's zebras.

These Grant's zebras live in Tanzania.

Mountain zebras are built more like donkeys, with long ears. Their stripes are thinner toward the front and wider toward the back. A flap of skin called a *dewlap* hangs down from their throats. There are two subspecies of mountain zebras. Hartmann's zebras have an off-white body with wide black stripes that go down the legs but not under the belly. They stand about 46 to 52 inches (117 to 132 cm) tall at the shoulder. Cape mountain zebras are the smallest zebras—about 47 inches (119 cm) tall. They're a little stockier than Hartmann's zebras, with longer ears. Their wide black stripes are set close together, with pure white stripes in between.

Mountain zebras' dewlaps are easiest to see on males.

Mountain zebras' hard, pointy hooves are good for climbing around in the mountains.

Hartmann's zebras make a sound like a horse neighing.

These Cape mountain zebras live in South Africa's De Hoop Nature Reserve. How do they differ from the zebra on page 7?

11

Grevy's zebras are especially rare. They're the largest zebras, and their long legs and slimmer build make them look different from the other two species. Adults are 55 to 57 inches (140 to 145 cm) tall at the shoulder and weigh 880 pounds (399 kg) or more. Their stripes are narrow and close together, running all the way down to their hooves. The stripes seem to form a bull's-eye pattern on the zebra's back end. Only the belly is white. Along the back, Grevy's zebras have a wide black stripe with a thin strip of white on each side. The ears are large and rounded, and the mane is long, with black-tipped hairs.

Grevy's zebras bray like donkeys.

Grevy's zebras are thought to be more closely related to wild asses than to other zebras.

There are only 5,000 to 10,000 Grevy's zebras left.

This Grevy's Zebra lives in Kenya's Samburu National Reserve. How does it differ from the zebras on pages 7 and 10?

How Do Zebras Live?

Plains zebras stay close and friendly by grooming each other. They lick and nibble each other's manes and necks to keep them clean.

Male plains zebras start their family herds by taking young females from other herds.

Zebras' ways of life depend on what kind they are and what part of Africa they live in. Plains zebras live mostly in the **savannas** of East Africa. They live in family herds. An adult male, or **stallion**, leads a group of several females, or **mares**, and their young. The stallion protects his herd from predators, staying behind to bite and kick as the rest of the group runs away. The oldest mares lead the herds as they move around to find food or water. Sometimes the family herds gather into much larger herds. Thousands of zebras might travel together, but within that huge group, each family herd stays close.

Here you can see a herd of Burchell's zebras grazing in Botswana's Chobe National Park.

Mountain zebras live in the mountainous grasslands and woodlands of southern and southwestern Africa. They live in small family herds, but these herds don't gather into huge groups like those of plains zebras.

Grevy's zebras live in deserts and dry grasslands of East Africa, especially northern Kenya. Well adapted to these drier areas, they don't need as much water as other zebras. Grevy's zebras don't form close family groups. Instead, a stallion claims a **territory** and marks it with his own smell. Then he tries to mate with mares that wander through it.

These two Grevy's stallions are fighting over a territory in Kenya.

Zebras have many ways of communicating with sounds and how they look. Baring their teeth is a way of saying hello. Pulling their ears flat back is a threat! Even how they hold their heads and tails has meaning to other zebras.

17

What Do Zebras Eat?

Zebras that live in zoos eat carrots, hay, and alfalfa.

Plains and mountain zebras have intestines 17 times as long as their bodies!

Most zebras need to drink water every day, so they stay within 3 to 6 miles (5 to 10 km) of water sources.

Zebras are plant-eating **herbivores** that spend up to 16 hours a day grazing. They eat over fifty different kinds of grasses, including tough, coarse grasses other animals won't eat. Often they're the first to start grazing in tall grasses. Once they've trimmed the grasses and trampled them underfoot, other herbivores such as gazelles and wildebeests join in. Zebras also sometimes eat leaves and stems of bushes.

Zebras have strong front teeth that snip plants off, and flatter back teeth that grind them up. Chewing tough plants wears down the zebra's teeth, but the teeth keep growing throughout the animal's life. Grasses aren't very **nutritious**, but the zebra's long, large body holds lots of this food while its stomach and intestines break it down.

This Burchell's zebra is munching on some grass in Zimbabwe.

Why Do Zebras Have Stripes?

To us, black and white stripes might seem to stand out from a background of grasses. But the zebra's main predators, lions, see only in black and white.

Some people think that zebras' stripes might confuse tsetse flies and keep them from biting.

Nobody knows for sure why zebras have such bright stripes, but people have some good ideas. First, the stripes break up the animal's shape, making it harder for a predator to see. The stripes might also help zebras blend in with tall grasses. Away from the grasses, they blend in with waves of heat rising from the plains. And when the zebras move in a herd, the stripes make it hard to tell one animal from another. That might confuse predators who want to pick out one zebra to attack. It would be especially confusing at dawn or dusk, when many predators are most active.

It's hard to tell where one of these Burchell's zebras stops and another begins!

20

Zebras' stripes are interesting in other ways, too. They're a lot like your fingerprints—no two zebra's stripes are alike! To tell two zebras apart, you need to look closely—especially at their shoulders, where the biggest differences occur. Stripe patterns help scientists who study zebras recognize certain zebras and keep track of them. And stripe patterns, along with smells, probably help zebras recognize each other. That would be a really big help when the zebras are in a large herd.

Look closely at these Burchell's zebras. Each one has a different stripe pattern!

Zebras like stripes! If a zebra sees black and white stripes painted on a wall or a piece of wood, it will stand next to them.

Zebras clean their coats by rolling in dust or mud. When they shake off the dirt, they also shake out old hair and little flakes of dead skin.

How Do Zebras Protect Themselves?

With their strong legs, zebras can run faster and farther than lions—up to 35 or 40 miles (56 to 64 km) an hour.

Zebras have been known to kill a hyena with one powerful kick.

If a zebra gets attacked and injured, its family forms a circle around it and protects it.

Zebras are always on the lookout for danger. They make good use of their keen eyesight and hearing. Since many predators hunt at night, zebras spend the night in open spaces where they can see. Zebras can see very well in the dark. In fact, they can see about as well as owls and cats.

For most zebras, living in family herds means that there are more animals to keep watch. At night, a herd's leader often sleeps standing up. Zebras often graze with other animals, such as wildebeests. Being in a larger group lessens the chance that any animal will be attacked.

These Burchell's zebras are gathering together as night falls on Kenya's Masai Mara Game Reserve.

What Are Baby Zebras Like?

Zebras can be born anytime during the year, but many are born in December and January—the early part of the rainy season.

Newborn zebras are brown and white.

A newborn zebra can stand and walk less than 20 minutes after it's born. Within an hour, it can run and drink its mother's milk.

About a year after mating, a zebra mare gives birth to a single **foal**. The newborn weighs 55 to 88 pounds (25 to 40 kg) and stands about 3 feet (1 m) high. The foal must get up and walk quickly—it needs to keep up with the moving herd. The mare keeps her foal away from other zebras for the first few days. That gives the foal time to learn to recognize its mother's stripe pattern, smell, and sound. The foal drinks the mother's milk for about a year. Zebra mares take good care of their foals. They do their best to protect them from hungry lions and hyenas. Even so, many foals are killed.

This Burchell's zebra foal is standing near its mother in Namibia's Etosha National Park.

Are Zebras in Danger?

In the wild, zebras can live to be about 20 years old. Under the care of people, they can live to 30 or more.

The quagga form of the plains zebra was killed off in the 1800s. Today, people in South Africa are trying to breed zebras that will look like the quagga.

People have hunted zebras for their meat and colorful skins, and because they sometimes compete with livestock for food and water. As human populations have grown, zebras have lost many of their living areas. Today, Grevy's zebras and Cape mountain zebras are **endangered**. Hartmann's zebras were endangered in the late 1900s, with only 7,000 left. They're doing a little better today—there are more than 15,000. Plains zebras have done even better, with probably 300,000 left in the wild. Even so, the number of plains zebras has dropped, and they're found in fewer areas.

Today, visitors to Africa love to see zebras. Many companies offer tours and safaris so people can see zebras running free. And governments are setting aside areas where zebras and other animals can live. If these efforts are successful, there will be zebras on the savanna for years to come!

28

This Cape mountain zebra lives in a national park in South Africa. There the zebra is protected from hunters and animal predators.

Glossary

endangered (in-DAYN-jurd) An endangered animal is one that is close to dying out completely. Grevy's and Cape mountain zebras are endangered.

extinct (ek-STINKT) An extinct animal or plant is one that has completely died out. The quagga went extinct in the late 1800s.

foal (FOHL) A foal is a baby horse. Zebra foals must be able to walk and run right away.

herbivores (HUR-bih-vorz) Herbivores are plant-eating animals. Zebras are herbivores.

mammals (MAM-ullz) Mammals are warm-blooded animals that have hair on their bodies and feed their babies milk from the mother's body. Zebras are mammals.

mares (MAIRZ) Mares are female horses. Zebra mares take good care of their babies.

nutritious (noo-TRIH-shuss) Nutritious foods have lots of substances that animals' bodies need to stay strong and healthy. Most of the grasses zebras eat aren't very nutritious.

predators (PREH-duh-terz) Predators are animals that hunt other animals for food. The zebra's main predator is the lion.

savannas (suh-VA-nuz) Savannas are grasslands with scattered trees and shrubs. Most zebras live in savannas.

species (SPEE-sheez) An animal species is a group of animals that share the same features and can have babies only with animals in the same group. There are three zebra species.

stallion (STA-lyun) A stallion is a male horse. Zebra family herds are led by a stallion.

territory (TEHR-uh-tor-ee) A animal's territory is the area that the animal claims as its own and defends against outsiders. Grevy's zebra stallions have territories.

To Find Out More

Watch It!

Families in the Wild—Zebras. Goldhil Home Media, 2001.

National Geographic Society. *Zebra: Patterns in the Grass*. VHS. Burbank, CA: Columbia TriStar Home Video, 1997.

Read It!

Anderson, Jill. *Zebras*. Minnetonka, MN: NorthWord Press, 2005.

Arnold, Caroline. *A Zebra's World*. Minneapolis, MN: Picture Window Books, 2006.

Stewart, Melissa. *Zebras*. New York: Children's Press, 2002.

Wexo, John Bonnett. *Zebras*. San Diego, CA: Wildlife Education, 1999.

On the Web

Visit our Web page for lots of links about zebras: *http://www.childsworld.com/links*

Note to Parents, Teachers, and Librarians: We routinely check our Web links to make sure they're safe, active sites—so encourage your readers to check them out!

Index